A Heart for the Home

Mending the brokenness in my heart.

Do Not open this testimony, unless you plan to change with me!

Sharise A. Caldwell

Copyright

Table of Contents

Dedication
Acknowledgements
A Note from the Author
Author's Tips
Who's the Author

Section I: Childhood pg10

Freebies, Goodies & Extras

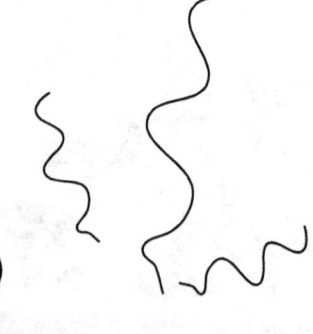

Dedication

    This book is dedicated to the Lord and Savior of my life, Jesus Christ. He is the reason I was able to organize my thoughts, recollect past memories, and fill this book with life giving words of hope, encouragement, and inspiration.

    I pray these stories and lessons guide you on your own journey to finding peace, self-love, wholeness, and boldness. You already have the courage to read. I pray you have even more for the next step in your faith walk.

Acknowledgements

I would like to thank my mom and dad for not only raising me but being supportive even when I first started out on my own two feet. Thank you, Mom, for instilling self-love and self-encouragement in me. Thank you, Dad, for sharing wisdom, giving me a different perspective, and always sharing my work with others. You two don't just say something; you actually put the action behind it. Thank you! Love you! Hugs & Kisses.

Here's a special 'thank you' to my husband and children for allowing me to grow, change, experiment, make mistakes, fail, give up, try again, be happy with success, and be disappointed with lack of progress. Thank you for always being there to support me through it all without ever complaining, crying, or showing fear. You guys are strong in spirit, wise beyond your years, and inspire Mommy to be her best self!

I can't complete this book without acknowledging all the special women who spoke into my life at the lowest times. I want to say 'thank you' to my coach, Patrice Cunningham Washington, for not just showing me the way but actually being a living and breathing example. 'Thank you,' Delisha Easley, for speaking into my life; I will never forget that moment. You changed my perspeception forever. 'Thank you,' Kenya Halliburton and Sonja Thompkins, for taking the time out to make me a better coach, business woman, and person.

Thank you to anyone who has ever supported me, including you readers, customers, clients, and fans! Thank you! You make it possible for me to continue to produce these special products.

A Note from the Author

All stories and memories are 100% true. In order to protect the integrity, dignity, and honor of my close relationships, I chose to leave names out of certain parts of this book.

When dark situations are being discussed in this book, it is explained enough for you to understand the main point but vaguely enough to keep material appropriate and Godly. Satan does not have an opportunity to use my past as bondage or evidence against anyone who may be involved.

All persons have been forgiven 10 years before this book was ever even thought about. I do not blame anyone or have negative feelings toward anyone. I am simply telling my whole truth as my testimony to help show others a way to heal, discover who they really are, and live a better reality for themselves.

You don't have to get stuck in the past. Accept what Christ has done on the cross and walk into a new life!

Author's Tips

Throughout the book the setting switches from authors' present to a piece of past memory. Actual conversations will be displayed like this:

> *This text box appears ONLY when it's a piece of past memory in story form, in addition to the italics for both to indicate a memory.*

To protect all parties involved, names, characters, and other ways to reveal identity have been presented respectfully. Some characters won't have names, instead the dialogue tag will say she, he, him, or her, for example.

Ex.	Person 1	*"Let's go outside." She said.*
.	Person 2	*"Ok!" He said.*
	Person 3	*"Do we have to?" She retorted.*
	Author	*"Can I come too?" The youngest child spoke.*

As author matures in age, characters will change, but the same principle still applies for that conversation whoever is talking will maintain their "name or phrase."

Who is the Author?

The answer to this question has changed 100X's since the first time I've personally asked myself. I thought I was clear about who I was (am). I never considered pausing for a moment everything I was doing to prove my identity in order to make sure it matched together. I was simply doing.

These next sections, chapters, and paragraphs are just pieces to my puzzle. I have yet to complete my whole story, because I am becoming every single day. I am constantly growing, being challenged, and discovering new things.

To you reader, if you feel these words beaming straight to your heart, then IT IS FOR YOU! I was her and am here to remember all things, whether good or bad, in order to connect with you. You are me when I was going through certain phases in my life. Your story may not be exactly like mine but we should be able to use what has been given to us,even if it was meant to stop, destroy, discourage, and take us away from God.

If you go through this with a willingness to cry, laugh, feel every emotion, receive every message, and then self reflect. You will take away a new perspective in hopes to write your own story in complete confidence that you matter. You can use it to help lift someone else up out there. That special someone is waiting for you to share your God given testimony.

YES! Let's be clear. You are NOT worthless, helpless, or hopeless. It is your time to heal, get clear direction, and to fulfill your true purpose.

Your Personal Encourager,

Sharise Caldwell

Section I:
Child Hood

1) Remember now thy Creator in the days of thy youth, while the evil days come not, nor the years draw and I, when thou shalt say, I have no pleasure in them;

13) Let us hear the conclusion of the whole matter: Fear God, and keep his commandments: For this is the whole duty of man.

14) For God shall bring every work into judgment, with every secret thing, whether it be good, or whether it be evil.

Ecclesiastes 12: 1, 13-14 (KJV)

> *"Heeelllpppp!" I sasid, yelling before taking my last breath.*
>
> *Panting. Puffing. Racing to get to me.*
>
> *"Somebody, help. She can't swim," My frantic mother panicked as she dropped everything to come and rescue me, her quiet, adventurous, currently drowning to death, babygirl. The most shocking part about this story is that it's just beginning.*

When I was little, I was a very sweet, petite cutie pie. I would quickly listen within the first given commands. I was quiet, peaceful, and not getting into a whole lot of trouble. I absolutely was a girly girl who didn't mind playing in the dirt.

Now before you say "Aww! She's an angel." These recollections are only from what I was told and not from my own perspective. I want you to relate to my whole experience to fully understand the entire story.

I was also told that I used to pick on my older brother. My brother and I are 4 years apart. Needless to say, I was your typical annoying little sister. Even worse in my case because I was the annoying little girl in my entire family.

How can someone so sweet be so aggravating? Easy! Just be born the youngest. Here is what I mean. My Sister is 10 years older. Most of my cousins we grew up with are closer to her age, not to mention the other ones who are even older than Big Sis. To my first point, I was too young to even know them. By the time I started opening my mouth to even say something, my age had already cancelled me from having the same experiences that my closest relatives were enjoying.

When I came around it was fun for me but more work for them. The funny inside jokes they secretly shared, the memories of summer time sleep overs. I was completely clueless of them all. Times had drastically changed when I was coming up in the 90's versus their familiar 80's era.

The little girl I was, squeezed right in between years of friendship, bonding, and uninterrupted laughter. Back then, each others' company was the entertainment. Especially when some uncles and aunties with strong personalities were thrown into the mix. It was hours of pure pleasure. So I get it. I was the uninvited one that had to stay anyways.

The little girl complex intensified as everyone grew older. I was no longer cute to pretend to play house anymore. I also became a direct target when all other avenues to express frustration were unavailable. I was the next best prey for anger, self hate, and relationship failure.

"Huuuhh. Huuuh. Huh. Huh. Huh.Huhh." I cried with tears overflowing from a sweet, Black, lonely little girl.
"Haha. Stop crying black baby." He said, meanfully.
" You a ugly little thing." The older child said agreeing with him.
" With your black gums." She said, being almost the same age as I.

A small group of kids but big enough to intimidate the little girl, circled around her. Enclosing the little girl with laughing, pointing, picking, and pushing, she had nowhere to escape. Her back was pinned against the bed in a tiny bedroom. The only thing left to do was cry because screaming may lead to more bullying.

" LEAVE ME ALONE" the little girl yelled for mercy!
" Ha ha. Ha ha haaaaa." He said.
" SHUT UP!" The older child said in annoyance.
" I hate when she says that. Let's just lock her in the room." One of the oldest children said.
"Great idea!" She said, who was the same age as me.

The door slammed shut trapping the little girl inside of the teeny weeny old creepy bedroom afraid, alone, and hated. Unfortunately, this became a ritual every summer. The bullying was mostly mental abuse. Strangely, over the years the little girl was gradually accepted in, but the damage was already done.

Ch. 2 *Grandma A.*

Everyone is getting older so fast, but I'm just beginning my journey. My mother came up with this grand idea for a family vacation to Walt Disney World. Her main reason for a once in a lifetime experience you would never forget, was to celebrate Big Sis before she completely left the nest.

We had such an amazing time! I remember tricking mom on to this elevator ride that went up a few stories high. It was called the Tower of Terror. Just so we are clear, it sounds as horrific as the name. It takes you up nice and slow while you are listening to the elevator operator tell a story. We were instantly transported into a historical scene full of unsolved mysteries. Out of nowhere the elevator loosens to take a free fall drop. We did not get back on that ride!

We all left vacation feeling ready for the new school year. I was entering second grade which turned out to be one of my most memorable school years. It is where I found my absolute favorite teacher of all times. Don't get me wrong. I did have more incredible, compassionate teachers who nurtured me and inspired me to continue a love of learning. There are too many to name. Thanks Ms. Susan, Ms. Jackson, and Ms. Harrison who made the most memorable impression on my young heart before life rudely interrupted.

My brother was in middle school and my sis was on her final year of high school. My parents working full-time had to make other arrangements once my sister graduated. She was so happy to begin her adult life while we were left behind to finish our own individual course.

For a little while we stayed with my grandma. We loved going over there mainly because she knew how to show love with her bomb food. This lady could whip up anything from memory and you already knew it was going to be delicious. She just had the magic touch when it came to making people feel invited, loved, and at home. Since she was my grandmother I was already home.

My grandmother tremendously helped with any request asked of her. She did above and beyond her normal duties. She was committed to serving others and living a quiet, peaceable, Christian life.

She meant so much to so many people, inside of the family church, but also to anyone who came across her path. She was one of the key people God sent in my life to show me the way I should eventually walk in. I didn't know it at the time that she was being led by God when she chose to take care of her family and community.

It is so sad that the perseption of a housewife or a woman who chooses to stay at home and work to keep the home functioning is deemed as stupid, useless, and poverish. These idiodic ideas strangled my thoughts towards my grandmother or any woman I would meet in my future who held this job title.

My grandmother would wake up early, start her day with coffee, cleaning, and worship music on the a.m radio gospel station. She would always have food around while preparing the main meal to eat for dinner. She was so gifted, no matter who sporadically popped in, she had enough prepared for all of us.

I may not have recognized how special she truly was to us. I may not have recognized that her job as grandma, mother, friend, and caregiver was extremely important. In fact, if she wasn't selfless and made herself available, so many people would have been left stranded, helpless, and without provision, including us.

We needed her to watch us after school, feed us dinner, and keep us whenever school was closed. I would later on realize just how much she already had done for me. I would much later realize just how much I needed her in my life.

I wished she was still around to teach me how to cook. I wished she was still around to share all the tips and tricks about keeping her home clean, organized, and tidy. I wished she was still around to tell me how in the world does she do it all by herself. I wished she was still here to, so I could hear her laugh, smell her cooking, and see her bright smile. Another significant moment thrusting me toward change was when she passed away in the fall of 2007.

Now who will hold our family together? I can't answer this question for you but if you're wondering how to be a better mother, wife, friend, boss, etc. Then I'm glad to tell you, this is exactly the reason why I kept creating resources to help you organize your life and business like *The Self Sufficient Housewife Calendar and Planner*. (Check details on page 52 for more info.)

" Can you please shut the door behind me." Mom shouted out so we can hear her over the rustling grocery bags held in her hands, along with a cell phone, purse, and other important work items.
"Mom." "Mom." Both children said, one right behind the other.
Mom started unpacking the food, began pulling out the pots and pans, plus changing into more comfortable clothing.
"Mooomm." He said with a rumble in his throat.
Mom continued preparations for tonight's dinner.
"Mommm, I really need to talk to you." He said as I was following in his footsteps.
"What would you guys like for dinner? I can make spaghetti or baked fish." Mom said as she continued preparation for tonight's dinner.
"MOM." He said with great annoyance.
"Yes son, I'm listening." Mom said leaning her ear forward to show attention to her son.

Another year has passed by, and we were almost at the age of mature teens. When I say we I really mean my brother. He was promoting to the ninth grade and felt he should also be allowed more freedom at home. He requested to begin staying at home alone, just him and his little sister (me.)

Of course I thought it was a dope idea. I would finally be able to make my own decisions and not look like a baby. My friends really didn't have strict rules. They were allowed to hang out with anyone, have sleepovers, and stay out late. It's not so bad talking about it now because I am also a mother who cares for the well being of her children.

Mild trauma came when I was treated like a little girl. So, this was a big deal to me the opportunity to stay home alone. I was left heartbroken to have to be excluded every single time because I was the youngest around. I needed my mom to say yes for me just this one time even if my brother was the one old enough to ask.

My parents decided it was time to give us more responsibility. I guess there wasn't a better time to be on our own considering we were only getting older and grandma deserved a break. Going to school, being home alone, watching tv, and playing outside became my new normal. None of it was bad until I began learning things my parents did not personally teach me or allow in our home.

I had such a strong passion for dancing that it was actually my lifelong dream. I was determined to become a famous dancer even if it was just a backup position. I honestly didn't care, as long as I was on stage with famous entertainers I idolized such as; Spice Girls, Brittany Spears, TLC, Destiny's Child, 3LC, and Aaliyah. I automatically assumed because of their fame people would know me, too.

I lived, breathed, and craved dance. For a while, I convinced everyone who came to know me, that I was surely going to make it in the industry one day. I failed to realize dance needed more than just a will to do it but discipline, critique, and a coachable spirit. Unfortunately, I did not possess these qualities at this time.

Oddly enough, mimicking the tv turned into desiring the same lives I admired. Young teens were often depicted in immature relationships, money, fame, sex, drugs, and alcohol. This list is what my heart desperately hoped for.

I, being naive, thought these qualities were considered desirable goals. Not just me but so many others around me. We fell right into a hole that would carry over into every area of our lives. These habits don't just go away when you hit a magical age of adulthood. ABSOLUTELY NOT. These learned behaviors need to be unlearned and at times uprooted by a great force, Christ and His Holy Spirit.

Although I was exposed to a lot of mature behaviors, even before staying home alone, it wasn't until I made somewhat of a conscious decision, that left me in a downward spiral.

I say somewhat conscious because I truly was innocent in

my thought making process. I was repeating learned behaviors that became habits which turned into strongholds. I honestly wasn't taught about certain situations that life would eventually present to me. My friends knew a whole lot more than I did and gladly passed their two cents my way.

My parents did not allow just any company to be around us, particularly me, their baby girl. Even in their best efforts and loving protection, I would soon fall into a deep, dark cycle that would have destroyed my entire life by the age of nineteen.

You will soon learn the most devastating dark moments I faced, God provided a way to escape, that eventually led me straight into His arms.

I noticed a pattern that turned into a vicious cycle. My household did not naturally have open or deep conversations. My parents were quiet, non-confrontational, and kept discussions age-appropriate.

My parents hid their adult oppositions away from us adolescents. I was so protected I didn't experience worry, heartache, or anxiety from normal life and adult stressors; like marriage, bills, and who will wash the dishes tonight?

Regrettably, keeping me away from life without replacing this ignorance with some type of informative understanding, I was just oblivious to the real world and easily fooled by other outside influences.

Whether we want to admit it or not, tv will raise our children if we are not setting the proper standards. It may seem right to not talk about certain subjects, but if I'm already being exposed to these adult topics, not appropriately, but as if I am ready to handle these ideas, then how are we truly protecting our children?

T.V., music, entertainment, and movies are exposing false truths and introducing abnormal topics at an early age. By not correcting what your child is watching or even absorbing we are doing ourselves a disservice.

How do we know our children are picking up these blatant messages? Have you ever wondered how come your child is acting a certain way so boldly and confidently? Where did he or she learn this idea from because you didn't teach it to them?

I usually say you are teaching them by not teaching them that this idea is wrong, removing the source that's causing the problem and replacing these ideas with the way of Christ.

My parents had a rough time with me because I wasn't consistently corrected and properly redirected. I had no respect for authority and needed a much stronger discipline enough to make me want to obey their instruction and honor their presence.

One major role parents have that has been strictly limited and down played by society is the power to influence their children to do good and not evil. The main idea is to give them more righteous choices than the distasteful behaviors they are naturally picking.

We may disagree with how we discipline and disciple our children, however, no one wants their child to suffer, struggle, and be in despair, if they could stop the harm from happening to them with simple correction, redirection, and structure. God gave you the power to stop them from unnecessary struggles in life. Will you use it?

If you're saying you agree with me but aren't quite sure how, than maybe Becoming More Beautiful program is for you (For more details check page 53).

Changed

"*What is it like to grow up?*" *I asked.*

"*I don't know. I haven't done it yet. But my brother is always up to something.*" *My best friend replied.*

"*Yeah, my brother gets to hangout all the time with his friends and I'm stuck here by myself. I wish I could just stay over your house at least until my parents get home.*" *I said dreaming it were true.*

"*My mom wouldn't care. She likes you. It would be perfect right after cheerleading practice.*" *My best friend said as she balanced on one leg with her arms out pretending to be a plane.*

"*It would be nice. Your cousin live right beside you, right?*" *I said with a smirk.*

"*Lol, he already has a girlfriend.*" *She said as she turned around to balance on the opposite leg.*

"*I know. I still want to get to know him.*" *I commented.*

"*Here you go again.*" *She said as she continued to be an airplane.*

"*It's not worse than you and your crush. Eww!*" *I responded with sas.*

"*I don't want to hear about another fantasy boyfriend you made up inside of your head. Just find someone who really likes you for you. Geesh!*" *She said with authority.*

Overwhelmed with unwelcomed sorrow again, within a few seconds apart, tears bum rushed me. I am struggling with some serious self esteem issues. Everybody in school is dating or at least has the option to reject an offer from a cute guy. I on the other hand is stuck in the single and ugly category all by my lonely desperate self.

I'm not very popular, not the smartest, but I make up for it with acting out in class and making everyone laugh. They love it when I talk loud, crack jokes, and be the class clown. I really don't have much of a choice. It's so boring. The lesson plans don't make sense and the teachers have awful attitudes. They have the nerve to say I'm the rude one.

Everyone knows you have to give respect to earn respect.

These teachers obviously missed the memo. It doesn't matter if I'm only in my pre-teen years, I deserve respect and will continue to act out until I get it. My parents disregard my sassiness so I'm just a ball of bad attitude walking around expecting everyone else to follow my orders.

By this time I officially hated going to school and was ready to finally be off on my own. I felt like I had to make stand alone decisions for my own benefit due to my chronological birth order, two working parents, and now staying at home alone more and more.

Even though I live in a loving home something was still off within me. I just felt like no one had the time to stop and give me attention. My sister has been gone for a few years now living her young adult life and starting her own family. My brother, well, he's in high school, will be the next child to graduate, and he's a boy. My parents still work full time to provide a better life for us.

I never understood why we didn't have more time together other than summer vacations. My parents never complained, just worked hard to take care of us, and they did a great job not exposing us to real life. No matter what problems they found themselves in, somehow, they just kept it together and kept it moving forward.

My decisions were completely foolish wrapped in a mirage and selfishness. I learned how to manipulate certain situations because for so long I was the one who would get the blame for everyone else's bad choices even when I was an honest child.

For so long I was the little girl and that meant the older kids could lie, cheat, and steal their way out of any problem. It didn't matter what happened. All they had to do was say I did it. Of course no one would protest their way into trouble on my behalf, even though it would have been the right thing to do.

In those critical years I needed my family the most to stand up for little ole' me. The truth is I didn't get that much needed alone time. I subconsciously craved, wished, hoped, and desired for intimacy. I was so angry with my family I wanted nothing else to do with them.

I really needed someone to set me down and say "Sharise, you don't have all the answers. You are not alone. Your family does love you. Have you considered their perspective other than your own point of view? What about your Mom? Dad? Sister? Brother? Don't they love you and care about you?"

If someone tried to change my young mind to get me to see my family as loving, working hard for my benefit, and that I truly had a great life. I would have replied, "Why am I left out?" The older I become my response would change to, "Oh, they don't count."

As I grow older I realize we all have issues and need to be our own detectives to find out if there is some hidden trauma disguised behind a bad attitude, working all the time, and simply not having a deep bond with our loved ones.

Being your own detective doesn't mean healing alone. It means you may have to decide you want to change your attitude, heal your relationships, and be a better you. You can go deeper into this self work with the companion journal, *A Beautiful Journey*.(For more details check page)

Children

My family was kind of mello and not really too involved in any drama. They were very hardworking people who came from more hardworking people. The times that we were together, hanging out, it was just that. To chill, kick back and have fun.

We didn't really have serious conversations, at least I wasn't invited to that particular table. I was a child, really about 11 years and younger. Of course I grew older but still I was the baby, will forever and always be the baby in my family.

This very curious ignorant child, without proper understanding about life, became my way of living. I responded to life with a child's mind. I responded with only my point of view. This one way thinking was truly detrimental to me and my household

Plenty of my life learned skills came from school, the neighborhood, and tv. My family didn't really talk much. We kept to ourselves. There was very little to no drama because we were peaceful people. Watching our words in conversations was a big part if not the sole reason as to why my family was so loving, kind, generous, and peaceful.

Staying in a child's place, not discussing certain topics, and without question, not speaking certain words like "liar" or the phrase "leave me alone." These lowly humble ways are not bad at all. They worked well and I myself have adopted a lot of those same principles, into raising my own children.

However, at some point, we didn't pass down important traditions. We didn't have proper family records, couldn't pass on information about family history, or be knowledgeable about practical Christianity. Prayer is super important but it also needs works to go with it.

I'm starting to realize that this is not just a family issue. As black people, we have part of the truth. Meaning, we have the basic needs, principles, and understanding to barely get by. My family as a whole were very beautiful people who did incredible things but were also greatly hindered from accomplishing even more because of part of the truth or just blatantly wrongful information.

Christ said "we would do greater." He also said "my people are destroyed for lack of knowledge." I have witnessed both. Greater in a sense that we had higher paying jobs, positioned ourselves into politics and government, lived in major cities, became homeowners, and kept in our right mindset to not live a life in the streets, like so many of our counterparts.

The lack of knowledge portion comes from many different places. We don't know who we are, where we come from, or where we're going. We don't know our purpose or the plans God has for us. We don't know how to think for ourselves. We don't know how to create generational wealth. And the list goes on.

How is this important little girl? This lack of knowledge led me to "figuring it out" on my own. How many of us live individual lives as best as we can? Sometimes we need each other. We can't do everything, all the time, on our own. It separates us and will lead to burn out, exhaustion, and a person operating from desperation and not their well rested selves.

We are born into families for a reason. Parents, children, adults and youth, we all have our own place because we all have unique gifts and talents even at those stages in life that if used properly will be a blessing and the answer to solve each other's problems.

This idea of separation has weakened us and slowly destroyed whole societies; it's a trickling effect. Parents too busy, unable to raise the children, arguing and fighting in their marriage, working "good" jobs, living bare minimal lives just doing the best you can, not taking risks. Not seeing the promises of God. Quoting every scripture but never experiencing the miracles, signs, wonders, and healings that are in there.

This lack that came from something so tiny has grown into a monster almost impossible to correct. Adults pass down information or a lack thereof to the youth. Doesn't matter if you're a bus driver, principal, manager, parent, sister, brother, friend, etc. Children grow to become adults. Adults become leaders. Adults have more children. It's a never ending cycle.

I will leave you with the problem and the solution.

> 6) *"My people are destroyed for lack of knowledge: because thou hast rejected knowledge, I will also reject thee, that thou shalt be no priest to me: seeing thou hast forgotten the law of thy God, I will also forget thy children."*
>
> Hosea 4:6

> 12) *"Verily, verily, I say unto you, He that believeth on me, the works that I do shall he do also; and greater works than these shall he do; because I go unto my Father.*
> 13) *And whatsoever ye shall ask in my name, that will I do, that the Father may be glorified in the Son.*
> 14) *If ye shall ask anything in my name, I will do it.*
> 15) *If you love me, keep my commandments.*
> 16) *And I will pray the Father, and he shall give you another Comforter, that he may abide with you forever;"*
>
> John 14:12-16

> 6) *"If any of you lack wisdom, let him ask of God, that giveth to all men liberally, and upbraideth not; and it shall be given him."*
>
> James 1:5

> 12) *"Let no man despise your youth; but be thou an example of the believers, in word, in conversation, in charity, in spirit, in faith, in purity."*
>
> 1 Timothy 4:12

Adults

$\mathcal{I}$ have had the most horrible victimized incidents occur to me and sadly it was adult workers in the school system that affected me the most. I have been verbally abused, put outside the classrooms, not allowed to use the restroom, yelled at closely in my face, and oh yeah, punished for being involved in bullying. Did I mention I was the one being bullied?

School did not favor me at all. I have to confess I did not treat adults with the respect they much needed and deserved. Respect should have been a no brainer to me. Seriously, you would think it was common sense, just cleaning up behind yourself before leaving the room.

I really didn't have responsibility in my home so I grew up thinking everything would be handed to me and everyone was at my disposal. Respect your elders little girl.

As a child I didn't know what I needed or what true love was. I would complain about having to do any chores in the house. I would complain about having to put my dirty dishes in the sink and wiping the table off.

The things I perceived as mistreatment, for example cleaning up, were really a twisted point of view which led to my outrageous and ridiculous behavior. My ignorance should not have been tolerated in my home because it caused a major problem with my attitude, how I felt towards adults and eventually prompted to rebellion.

I used to blame my parents because I thought they were responsible for my actions. I thought they should be blamed for me not listening, doing as I was told, or my lack of being kind. My mother would often tell me "It doesn't hurt to be kind." Underneath my breath I would negatively respond "yes it does."

Can we all agree that at some point I should have been corrected? There is such controversy over, whether or not parents should be able to discipline their own children. The proof is comparing a child who isn't disciplined and is allowed to disrespect their elders to children with proper correction and redirection from their guardians. How do their actions and results differ?

I remember very distinct times that changed my outlook on school, education, goals, and teachers. Another incident was in third grade. I received my first C. I remember crying the rest of the day because I felt like a failure. I knew I could do better. I felt insulted against my character. The issue was the planned lessons were moving too quickly, I didn't understand the work, or have time to actually learn the material. I didn't even have time to memorize the work. It had nothing to do with my character at all even though my teacher was very hostile against me as if I had a disciplinary issue.

A group of highschoolers came to our classroom as student helpers. They were the nicest people to show me that school could be fun. If it wasn't for them volunteering I would have never remembered my multiplication facts. I was a little more confident because I did score higher on the 100 questions in 1 minute timed test. I was finally able to prove to one of the meanest teachers I had, that I was precious, valuable and had worth.

One incident in fifth grade this teacher was known for being extremely nasty. It was weird because her husband was one of the most loveable teachers in the entire intermediate school.

I had her for one year in math class. She told us we could not go to the bathroom in her classroom at all the entire year. I was so afraid to even ask to go to the bathroom I literally had an accident on myself. She took me outside the classroom, asked me why I didn't say anything, and labeled me as someone who needed "special attention." I was allowed to go to the bathroom from then on but I was so humiliated.

The last incident I will share will be in another teacher's fifth grade class-room. She too was known to be wicked. She got so fed up with me talking in class she moved my desk facing the wall as a separation form the rest of the students. I chose to talk to myself out loud in the corner as long as I was permitted. When this tacktick didn't work she actually put my desk outside of the classroom. Of course I found a way to entertain myself: when students walked by I spoke to them.

Usually it was the female teachers that were out of control in their behavior. When the special-ed class would join ours, both teachers would be yelling at both sets of students uncontrollably. This type of bullying was a trigger for me because I could never understand why you would pick on someone smaller than you, innocent, and in this particular case, having a disability.

I really didn't like adults for these core reasons. Plus, whenever my parents were involved, usually I was ridiculed and my parents were tricked into believing the other side. I was left defenseless and looking like a trouble maker yet again.

The hateful adults were abusive, manipulating, selfish, mean, non-caring, impatient, and just rude. How can you hate people that much, especially children? Weren't adults children too? Or are we two separate species?

These are only a few incidents that I will share. My angle is not to bash or shame any individual because we all make mistakes and we all do according to what we know. With that said many of these people were responding to life. It wasn't their normal default. It's something they developed overtime.

It's the same thing that happened to me. Children do not stay kids for long. Soon they will be grown adults with the same flaws, issues, bad attitudes, and zero respect for other people.

This is an ongoing endless cycle that is creating a huge problem. If there is war between the old and young I want to be the person to bridge the gap and make peace.

The truth is we need both the old and the young. The old are wise and the young are fearless. With both we can do the impossible.

Disappointedly, it took me years to realize I needed guidance from my peers. No matter how flawed the adults were around me, learning from their mistakes and giving them respect would have been better than growing up with resentment trying to prove everyone else wrong.

It affected how I showed up in relationships. It drove me to easily give up and move on to the next thing.These experiences went wounding my heart and began to pierce my soul.

"MOM. DAD. TEACHER. Where are you?"

Bad

$\mathcal{I}$ have to say, looking back, I caused a lot of conflict in my own relationships. I had a smart mouth, would act in self-defense, and was always ready to prove a point.

The phone calls home would result in my parents being frustrated with me but not fully understanding the entire story. Usually, the story was only a one-sided conversation making me out to be the villain and not the victim. This was purposely miscommunicated causing me to get in trouble.

I had to forgive a lot of adults that in my opinion, should have known better. Adults that wanted to seek revenge on children. I was acting out until acting out became the only way of escape. The only way to demand and receive proper treatment from others.

I didn't know it at the time, but I was dealing with trauma, fear, and false labels from wrongful accusations and misperceptions of me. My parents were deceived into these hideous lies as well. I mean really. Who would believe a child over an adult's statements?

Certainly not the school itself. Let me remind you of my little history with older, more mature children. Mmmhmm, they finessed their testimonies to work in their favor, which was the complete opposite of mine. It was their dishonesty over my honesty.

Time and time again I was made out to be the problem child before I even intentionally caused major problems. It's a difference from being messy and young compared to deliberately picking on others, destroying property, and just being bad.

I went from innocent to being bad unapologetically. My parents deserved so much better in life from what they were given. I wish my mind could understand their humble peaceful spirits. I had war raging inside of my heart towards them, when all they had to give was unconditional love. This is what I would need later on to come back home to.

I needed a different kind of love that would listen to my greatest concerns. A love that could tell me "NO" when I was wrong. A love that could correct my bad attitude. A love that could have meaningful conversations that would silence my questions and fears. A love that I could escape to for safety and peace.

Don't get me wrong. There were plenty of fond times we had as a family. The problem was I was just too young to remember. My memories would be overtaken, changed, and completely ruined by the current situations I was having.

No one knew what I saw, heard, been around, or what was even introduced to me. I can clearly see why these things happened when I was young. Two main recurring themes that bred inappropriate behavior in children that should be exclusive to adults with mature minds are; 1) Children who were left alone 2) Children who was exposed to adult content.

All these incidents that somehow involved me at a young age was to destroy my character as who God created me to be. A piece of me significantly altered as each case progressed in my life until finally the depletion of who I was occurred. I was not the same sweet, quiet or innocent little girl anymore.

For now on, everyone who mistreats me will be mistreated back. I will not be victimized any longer. It is up to me to stand up for and take care of myself.

I believe this is why I was so passionate about being popular and becoming everyone's friend. I wanted people to like me. I now had the courage and know how to get the results I wanted. So why not use this power for good, by being a friend to the outcast and for standing up for the ones without voices?

Sure I'm mean, nasty, and arrogant, but I can use my power to avenge the other's like me.

Tiny Town

My parents would leave for work while we were asleep, and come back home just in time to fix dinner and head to bed. They supported each of us in pursuing our interests. My sister was a cross country champion. My brother was a natural talent for gymnastics. And then there was me.

By the time I came of age a lot of these programs were completely gone and it would be nearly impossible to find other places and impossible to find transportation to those places. Plus, add that additional cost on our monthly expenses, girl you can forget about it.

The tiny town mindset consists of a number of things. 1) There are little to no opportunities for growth. 2) Once there, always there. 3) You're lucky to get a job. 4) If you have a job it's most likely low paying. 5) Racism wasn't prevalent because of old segregation lines. Meaning the old way had a way to still exist just without saying so.

When I was growing up black, I would hear and see minor things but pay no attention to them. I thought some people were just mean, rude, and had a bad attitude. I couldn't understand why certain people looked at me with disgust or didn't want me around their children.

My neighbors in particular allowed one black family to visit them as long as that family acted to their standards. This was always hard for me to comprehend for two main reasons. Reason number one. My parents were very nice and respectful people. Reason number two. That accepted black family was still "Black."

How come we were told not to play together? Color wasn't talked about around me at all. As far as I know, I'm just a normal girl. I went to a pool every summer and hadn't had the slightest clue of its history. I wouldn't find out until many many years later that I was going to the "black pool." The white pool was still up and running as well, but hidden under a new name, "private."

No wonder there were very few light complected families swimming with us.

  This was not the only incident. I was suspended in second grade because of a girl saying very cruel racist words to me. Although she was also in second grade, she was much taller, wider and could easily hurt me. I don't know why this really upset and provoked me to anger, knowing we wasn't taught to think this way at home.

  I immediately got revenge the next time we were allowed to use the restroom. I took my anger out on her by getting in her face and raising my voice to say mean words back to her. Being way smaller than she was, I chose to intimidate the girl by picking her up against the wall. To my surprise, it worked! I had the strength to pin her against the wall and to scare her off, never bullying me again.

  I was instantly reported and in trouble for a long time even though it was self-defense. By nature, I usually am the smallest person in the room. That doesn't mean I can't be dangerous, true. But what about self-defense?

  I have been lied upon various times, physically bullied, intimidated, and just without adult supervision or help. Usually when I told or if the other parties involved told their lies, I would be the only person getting in trouble.

  I was utterly fed all the way up and sick of the lies. Why continue to allow people to use me as a target? I became so frustrated it turned into bitterness towards people in general, kids as well as adults. I was coming for everybody and they mama, too!

  It's one thing to stand up for myself against other children. However, I have no right to try and put adults into their places. It became very difficult for me to listen, trust, or even care about an elder's opinion. If you were an adult and did not stick up for me, you were on my disrespect list.

Discipline

There is major confusion around the topic of disciplining our children. We believe we are helping our kids by allowing them to do any and everything they want to do.

We believe we are showing them love by accepting who they are. In reality, we are creating the very beings they are becoming, whether good or bad. They are human beings that will produce love or evil.

Children are somehow put into separate people groups as if we all did not start off as a child. Didn't we have feelings, personalities, and talents? Children are sensitive and extremely intelligent human beings just in smaller packages.

Parents are not the blame for everything their children do, however, we do play a major role in what they perceive as truth. Their truth is how they will respond and express themselves in life. Their truth is what they will become.

Do you know your children enough to predict the choices they will make? Do you know your children enough that if you have more than one child you know exactly who did what based upon the evidence and just being in tune with who they are?

This is a great start but there is more. Instead of passing it off like you don't know where they are getting this behavior from, this is the perfect time to be actively correcting, instructing, and redirecting them because we need this direction on a consistent basis.

Why and how you ask? It's quite simple! Let me explain. If I give my child candy they will expect it, unless I made it clear it was only for that one time or for a special occasion. If they decide to ask, that's fine, I will re-state that it was just for that particular time and stay grounded in that decision.

It's just candy right. What can it hurt? What's the big deal? If I don't establish healthy habits now it will quickly get out of my control and harm the both of us in the end.

Let's keep with the example above. Too much candy may

cause severe tooth decay, gum disease, tummy aches, diabetes, sugar addiction, poor appetite, and obesity, just to name a few side effects.

It's easier to say *NO* with confidence when we slow down and consider the consequences for allowing certain behaviors to continue to develop in our children. It's our responsibility to set the standard as parents especially when they are at the age of living in our homes and under our care.

There is no age requirement to start teaching healthy habits, establishing clear rules, and keeping godly boundaries. The sooner you instill values inside of your children the better. There is a time where the grace of teaching them your principles will come to an end.

Then they are who they are. You have to love them from a distance because they will operate in the environment you have previously allowed them to nurture and grow in. If it doesn't bother you NOT to raise your children according to God's commandments, then this simply doesn't apply to you.

I was the babygirl, *true*, but that doesn't automatically mean my parents should have to baby me for the rest of my life. At a certain age, the disrespect should have been dealt with. Discipline or punishment does not have to be abusive at all, just a clear direct order of correction because when there is no order the child, believe it or not, will grow up not knowing how to be a respectful responsible adult.

Naturally, parents are the first teachers about life, relationships, and God. I wasn't taught to respect my elders in a way it was dire and urgent. I didn't have to take responsibility at home with daily chores. I also was rejecting the obvious responsibilities I had as a daughter.

I was breaking down on the inside because I wanted someone to rescue me from my own self-caused problems but didn't understand that rules were the answer to my turmoil. I needed guidelines, direct commands, and authority to help keep my honest, sweet, and obedient spirit alive.

We had rules but little by little lost the sincerity and respect for these rules. Some of these rules I ignored at home, I later on had to follow when I was a guest over someone else's home or else

I would not be allowed to come back(which happened more often than a sincere invite.).

The rules were beneficial, if and when, we followed them. So where was all of the friction really coming from? Not having accountability and trying to do things alone.

I Thought

"What's wrong with you? My mother said as she spoke up for herself against my rebellion.

What's wrong with you? I said, but only inside of my mind so she couldn't hear it.

"Why are you acting like this?" My mother said, questioning her best efforts to be a good mom.

Why are you acting like this? I said inside of my mind again, but a little sassier. She still couldn't hear me though, but it felt good anyways just to say what I was feeling.

"I mean I don't get where we went wrong with you?...."

My thoughts cut my other off as she was having a heartfelt conversation with me to plead a truce. "I know the answer to your stupid question. I know the answer to everything. I always know the answer, it's you guys who just isn't listening." I paused my thoughts from ranting on to only realize that I wasn't the one listening to my concerned mother. If I would have paused more often maybe I would have had a better respect for my hardworking devoted parents. This moment I paused just in time to actually hear a glimpse of what she was trying to communicate throughout the length of our relationship.

"Your father and I work hard to give you a better life so you would have everything you need and not have to ask for anything. We don't ask you guys to do much of anything around here....." My mother said, earnestly.

This was unexpected to me because she never opens up to her kids about her mommy responsibilities; she just does them. Both of my parents do.

Sometimes I felt bad for the harsh feelings I actually had against my own house and then I remembered how I tried to do as I was told, but for some odd reason, Sharise was the blame for it all.

By now I kept secrets to myself. I didn't trust anyone and the people who were in close proximity were the very people who betrayed me. Only a handful of strangers and acquaintances took advantage of my friendliness and assumed I was easy to fool. Well, they were right every time. I was ignorant to a lot of things until they were introduced to me.

I never shared somethings i witnessed. I didn't know how to share these secrets or just wanted to hide them. I treated my parents as if they should "just know" as a typical wife assumes of her husband when barking orders.

These learned behaviors later on turned into a reckless way of living as a means to cover up my true emotions inside but also to gain the attention I was desperately craving for.

$\mathcal{A}$ lot of the problems I was facing came from others outside of my immediate family. A lot of problems were close friends, extended family members, and even people around the neighborhood I grew up in.

I understand now my parents are not all-knowing or all-seeing. But back then, in my little eyes, they were my everything. They were supposed to save me from all of life's problems.

They were supposed to be my best friends. They were supposed to show me how valuable I was, especially when I became a teen. They were supposed to introduce me to the only one being that could be there whenever I needed Him to be.

And they did just that! My parents often had to wake-up so early in the morning that it would be a couple of hours before the sun rose just so they could drive, bumper to bumper, in city traffic, in order to make it to work on time at a decent paying job with benefits.

I didn't realize many things when I was a child; I thought everybody should share the same opinions as I did. I thought my parents were to blame for everything. I thought no one in my entire family could do anything right including, loving me. I thought I had to be bad to compete with bad behaviors of my influencers. Lastly, I thought I had to defend myself against the world.

I didn't realize the negative outside influences my parents tried to protect me from snuck into my heart. All the rules I didn't want to follow, all of the constant direction, all of the repeated instructions, expectations, and church functions were for my good, I just didn't know.

There were so many indicators that something was becoming a serious problem within my spirit. The lack of miscommunication, misunderstanding, and me as a child not knowing how to handle trauma or even be able to recognize that I was having a traumatic experience left me broken and bitter.

Sure we can ignore the signs that our children need a little more attention, structure and discipline in their lives, but if we're honest with ourselves we know this will soon lead to more chaos and destruction.

The Truth

The truth is that our children are constantly learning. We all are evolving into something different each and every day. Will we evolve into something greater than our previous moment? Or will we gravitate backwards into a worse condition than the moment now?

Our children are being bombarded with outside influences that are trying to breach deep into their souls. Satan doesn't need a personal invitation, if the door inside of their hearts or minds is slightly cracked, he gladly takes his opportunity to welcome himself inside of what he now sees as his home. Satan doesn't play fair in anything. He only lies, cheats, and tricks his way into stealing, killing, and utterly destroying. There is no good deal when your dealing with satan, demonic activity, or sin.

This place inside of hearts is not for satan or our own selfish desires, it is solely for Almighty God. This is why Christ died on the cross to take the place of judgement for us. He fulfilled the law (obeyed the rules his parents gave) for people who tried their best but still dropped the ball in life.

My parents are the nicest people on the planet but got stuck with a rebellious child like me. Christ needed to be primary in our home for my very sake. They had the rule. They followed the rules. Under the assumption this was enough to raise God fearing children, I was oblivious to what the rules meant, why we did what we did and Christ WHO?

When I say Christ who, it isn't because I have never heard of his name before. It isn't because I didn't ever go to church. It isn't because my parents didn't act Christ like. It's because I personally didn't know Him like I was familiar with my mom, dad, sister, and brother.

Good and evil will always be here as long as we are living and breathing in this world. The catch is, if we aren't constantly practicing and being intentional, over and over and over again about good behavior, then being bad will continue to rule in our lives. Once you know it's wrong, then it is counted as sin. Nothing good comes from sin, things only grow worse.

When I say good behavior I mean having morality, standards, and values. We can argue about who's right and who's wrong until the truth is present. Once the truth is here, whichever side is opposite of the truth is in the wrong. At this point it's not right or wrong anymore its what is the truth and what is the lie?

Some of these arguments come from how we feel and not the whole truth. This is why God's word (The Holy Bible, KJV) is so crucial for us to read until we have understanding. When you understand what the scriptures are saying you can adopt these teachings (rules) in your home.

These disciplines may not feel good like eating vegetables but they are more important. Eating your vegetables keep your body strong but reading the bible keeps your spirit healthy. When your spirit is healthy your character is better. When your character is better you can make better choices, decisions, and judgements that will save you from unnecessary problems.

It's crucial for our mental health. It's crucial for our inner healing. It's crucial in marriage to keep it unified and on the same page. It's crucial for how to raise your children. It's crucial for confronting your own sin.

Ladies, you have more authority, control, and influence than you even knew about. You have authority as a mother. You have control when it comes to how you want to live your life and with whom. You also have influence as a woman when you tap into your feminine beauty.

This femininie power can be used in all of the titles and positions you posses to either bring positive impact or a negative result. You choose. If you feel powerless, hopeless and discouraged, maybe *Affirmations for a Beautiful Heart* can help! (For more info check page 52)

Your title as Mom, Wife, fill in the black to other positions such as CEO, has already given you the upper hand. The only thing left to do is walk in your authority, be confident in God's word, and trust His provision in your life as guardian for your home.

Guardian means defender, protector, keeper. Are you doing

these things for the people inside of your house? Are you acting this way for your friends, co-workers, other family members other than for your spouse and children?

My parent's did introduce these truths to me early on. They did everything they knew was right. We didn't just go to church, but we came home, prayed at home, and lived out Christian lives to the best of our abilities.

With all of their effort, the love they provided was inundated by outside influences penetrating into the walls of our home by attaching its ideologies on the people who lived in the house.

My parents good character, morals, values, and rules became old, outdated, overpowered and replaced by other things. My parents are lovely sweet people but I still faced serious issues. Their only hope was God. My only hope became God.

I grew up in a culture with churches all around. Going to church on Sundays was tricky for us because we had to drive long distance just to get to the church my parent's belonged to. What a great experience for them and us kids. So many fun memories with music, dancing, singing, and yummy snacks.

Through my experience, being inconsistent with going to church and having personal bible study at home,was the downfall. My memory of this church stopped at 5 years old.

If we stopped eating what would happen? Eating can be paused for fasting but only for a short period of time, even if it is for forty days. Forty days compared to the rest of your life is a short time frame.

Having a true relationship with Jesus Christ and following His instructions is equivalent to eating. We need to eat so we need Him more! He is the Bread of Life. Without Him everything else that is feeding us or getting our attention is equivalent to junk, non-nutritional food; it fills you up but with no nutritional value.

Introducing God as a real living being that we can be in true relationship with is the key to solving everything I discussed in this book.

Living out our relationship with Christ as women is more than just do's and don't (rules,chores, etc.). Living out our faith can be practical and easy enough that a child can mimic.

At first it may be children doing what their parents told them. These learned behaviors with the power of prayer and God should turn our actions from doing what we are told to doing what we sincerely want to do.

I used to love going to church. I wasn't rebellious against authority. I learned how to do what I wanted to do for my own gain without considering others.

A child can fall in love with and continue to follow Christ at a young age even when the parents aren't around. A child can learn how to do good because he or she was taught, consistently(nutritional food for the spirit).

When I wasn't in church on a regular basis due to the traveling time, I began to forget. Later on, as I got older, I started to make my own choices, but still with a corrupted child's mind. The decision to not listen and honor the rules given to a child is a major issue that parents have the duty and responsibility to protect. When the child becomes of an age of understanding right from wrong, that's when it is counted as their choice and not left as guilt on the parents.

I did a lot of things out of pure ignorance because these concepts were not broken down into small bite size pieces I could practice daily to have it become a part of me. It was a list of Do's and Don'ts, that I honestly didn't comprehend the reason for the rules. I took it personally and thought I was being singled out and picked on like the black sheep of the family. Unfortunately, I felt I only had the DO NOT list when my older siblings and cousins had the better of the two sides.

This left me feeling mistreated, unrewarded, and resentful because I would watch someone get rewarded for bad behavior when I was truthful, quiet, wouldn't bother anyone and would follow directions. Bye-bye- Ms. Nice Girl. Hello, Ms. Bad Attitude!

I Need More

Thank you so much for reading this book! We've been through so much together, especially, if you have been on your own journey using *A Beautiful Journey*.

This book may have been short, sweet and straight to the point but the story isn't over yet. Part II will be releasing very soon. Be sure to get on our email list so you will be notified first.

I wrote my entire story when I heard the Lord say "Write the book." I did as He instructed even though I had no clue what He was even talking about.

After I wrote what was surprisingly inside of me, I sent the book to be edited by Cassidy A. Lee. My beautiful editor suggested the book to be split into three parts and I couldn't agree more. So if you're looking for more, want more, and need more check out the companion journal, where ever you purchased this book.

In addition to the amazing book and it's journal, we have a beautiful set of affirmation cards that you can easily transport with you, while you are on the go!

If you're saying, "Sharise all that is good but I still need more." I invite you to sign up for the group coaching program, Becoming More Beautiful. I can't wait to welcome you in this new season.

If you're saying, " Sharise I would love to join but now isn't the right time." No problem love. Join the 5 day free challenge, *Make me Over Again.*

If you're saying I want more more, subscribe to *My Beautiful Book Boss* the podcast!

Whatever you do next, just do the next best step for you!!!!

These programs are seasonal so be sure to sign up while you can when it is being promoted. To check all current promotions visit www.ShariseAntionette.com

Also stay connected on our social media platforms, of your choice.

May you be blessed by this book for many years to come, write a review, plus post it so another sis can join in the movement.

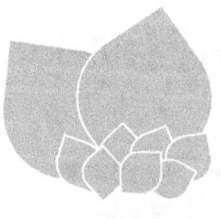

Scriptures by Topic

Parent and child relationship:

John 9:20 His parents answered, "We know he is our son, and we know he was born blind.

Hebrews 11:23 By faith Moses, when he was born, was hid three months of his parents, because they saw he was a proper child; and they were not afraid of the king's commandment.

Luke 2:41-45 Now his parents went to Jerusalem every year at the feast of the passover.
And when he was twelve years old, they went up to Jerusalem after the custom of the feast.
And when they had fulfilled the days, as they returned, the child Jesus tarried behind in Jerusalem; and Joseph and his mother knew not *of it*.
But they, supposing him to have been in the company, went a day's journey; and they sought him among *their* kinsfolk and acquaintance.
And when they found him not, they turned back again to Jerusalem, seeking him.

Luke 8:41-42, 55-56 And, behold, there came a man named Jairus, and he was a ruler of the synagogue: and he fell down at Jesus' feet, and besought him that he would come into his house: for he had one only daughter, about twelve years of age, and she lay a dying. But as he went the people thronged him.
And her spirit came again, and she arose straightway: and he commanded to give her meat.
And her parents were astonished: but he charged them that they should tell no man what was done.

Scriptures by Topic

Parent and child relationship:

Colossians 3:20 Children, obey *your* parents in all things: for this is well pleasing unto the Lord.
Fathers, provoke not your children *to anger*, lest they be discouraged.

Ephesians 6:1-4 Children, obey your parents in the Lord: for this is right.
Honour thy father and mother; which is the first commandment with promise;
that it may be well with thee, and thou mayest live long on the earth.
And, ye fathers, provoke not your children to wrath: but bring them up in the nurture and admonition of the Lord.

2 Corinthians 12:14-15 Behold, the third time I am ready to come to you; and I will not be burdensome to you: for I seek not your's, but you: for the children ought not to lay up for the parents, but the parents for the children.
And I will very gladly spend and be spent for you; though the more abundantly I love you, the less I be loved.

2 Timothy 3:1-2 This know also, that in the last days perilous times shall come.
For men shall be lovers of their own selves, covetous, boasters, proud, blasphemers, disobedient to parents, unthankful, unholy,

1 Timothy 5:4 But if any widow have children or nephews, let them learn first to shew piety at home, and to requite their parents: for that is good and acceptable before God.

Scriptures by Topic

Parent and child relationship:

John 9: 1-3, And as *Jesus* passed by, he saw a man which was blind from *his* birth.
And his disciples asked him, saying, Master, who did sin, this man, or his parents, that he was born blind?
Jesus answered, Neither hath this man sinned, nor his parents: but that the works of God should be made manifest in him.

John 9:18-23 But the Jews did not believe concerning him, that he had been blind, and received his sight, until they called the parents of him that had received his sight.
And they asked them, saying, Is this your son, who ye say was born blind? how then doth he now see?
His parents answered them and said, We know that this is our son, and that he was born blind:
but by what means he now seeth, we know not; or who hath opened his eyes, we know not: he is of age; ask him: he shall speak for himself.
These *words* spake his parents, because they feared the Jews: for the Jews had agreed already, that if any man did confess that he was Christ, he should be put out of the synagogue.
Therefore said his parents, He is of age; ask him.

Luke 18:28-30 Then Peter said, Lo, we have left all, and followed thee.
And he said unto them, Verily I say unto you, There is no man that hath left house, or parents, or brethren, or wife, or children, for the kingdom of God's sake,
who shall not receive manifold more in this present time, and in the world to come life everlasting.

Scriptures by Topic

Parent and child relationship:

Romans 1:28-32 And even as they did not like to retain God in *their* knowledge, God gave them over to a reprobate mind, to do those things which are not convenient;
being filled with all unrighteousness, fornication, wickedness, covetousness, maliciousness; full of envy, murder, debate, deceit, malignity; whisperers,
backbiters, haters of God, despiteful, proud, boasters, inventors of evil things, disobedient to parents,
without understanding, covenantbreakers, without natural affection, implacable, unmerciful:
who knowing the judgment of God, that they which commit such things are worthy of death, not only do the same, but have pleasure in them that do them.

Proverbs 17:6 Children's children *are* the crown of old men; And the glory of children *are* their fathers.

Deuteronomy 24:16 The fathers shall not be put to death for the children, neither shall the children be put to death for the fathers: every man shall be put to death for his own sin.

Proverbs 31:1-3 The words of king Lemuel, the prophecy that his mother taught him.
What, my son? and what, the son of my womb? And what, the Son of my vowels

Isaiah 54:13 And all thy children *shall be* taught of the LORD; and great *shall be* the peace of thy children.

Scriptures by Topic

Parent and child relationship:

Proverbs 1:8-9 Hear, my son, your father's instructions, and forsake not your mother's teaching, for they are a graceful garland for your head and pendants for your neck."

Psalm 127:3 "Children are a gift from the Lord; they are a reward from him.

Matthew 19:14 But Jesus said, Suffer little children, and forbid them not, to come unto me: for of such is the kingdom of heaven.

3 John 1:4 I have no greater joy than to hear that my children walk in truth.

Deuteronomy 5:29 O that there were such an heart in them, that they would fear me, and keep all my commandments always, that it might be well with them, and with their children forever!

Matthew 18:1-3 At the same time came the disciples unto Jesus, saying, Who is the greatest in the kingdom of heaven?
And Jesus called a little child unto him, and set him in the midst of them,
and said, Verily I say unto you, Except ye be converted, and become as little children, ye shall not enter into the kingdom of heaven.

Deuteronomy 6:6-7 And these words, which I command thee this day, shall be in thine heart:
and thou shalt teach them diligently unto thy children, and shalt talk of them when thou sittest in thine house, and when thou walkest by the way, and when thou liest down, and when thou risest up.

Scriptures by Topic

Parent and child relationship:

Jeremiah 1:5-7 Before I formed thee in the belly I knew thee; and before thou camest forth out of the womb I sanctified thee, and I ordained thee a prophet unto the nations.
Then said I, Ah, Lord GOD! behold, I cannot speak: for I am a child.
But the LORD said unto me, Say not, I am a child: for thou shalt go to all that I shall send thee, and whatsoever I command thee thou shalt speak.

Psalms 139:15-16 My substance was not hid from thee,
When I was made in secret, *and* curiously wrought in the lowest parts of the earth.
Thine eyes did see my substance, yet being unperfect; And in thy book all *my members* were written, *Which* in continuance were fashioned, When *as yet there was* none of them.

Psalm 139:13-14 For thou hast possessed my reins: Thou hast covered me in my mother's womb.
I will praise thee; for I am fearfully *and* wonderfully made: Marvellous *are* thy works; And *that* my soul knoweth right well.

Proverbs 29:17 Correct thy son, and he shall give thee rest; Yea, he shall give delight unto thy soul

Mark 10:15-16 Verily I say unto you, Whosoever shall not receive the kingdom of God as a little child, he shall not enter therein. And he took them up in his arms, put *his* hands upon them, and blessed them.

Connect with Us

We are passionate about serving the community we are building. Get connected to like minded women of faith with My Beautiful Book Boss The Movement (Private FaceBook Group).
Come and enjoy real conversations by streaming our Podcast, available to download on all platforms: My Beautiful Book Boss

     ♥ **Have** a business, organization, non-profit, book, podcast, or YouTube connect with us for collaboration and networking opportunities.
     ♥ **Have** a story of your own and have the heart to share it with us, there maybe spots available to be a special guest on our social media series.
     ♥ **Have** a course or book and would like us to design, format, and layout a workbook or journal as an addition to your brand.
     ♥ **To support** our brand, mission, and movement become a sponsor today!

♥ ♥ ♥ Please fill out our contact form, which can be found on our website below, for any of the following inquiries mentioned above: www.shariseantionette.com ♥ ♥ ♥

To stay up to date on future products, Like and Follow our social media pages below.

YouTube Channel: Sharise Caldwell
Instagram: @shariseantionette
Twitter: @sharisecaldwell
Linked In: Sharise Caldwell
Facebook: @MyBeautifulBookBoss
Facebook Community Group:
MyBeautifulBookBossThe Movement

More Products

Be on our email list for the upcoming releases, specific dates will be announced soon:

Fall 2023
- ❤A Heart for the Home Part II Young Adulthood: Mending every area of Brokenness in my Relationships

- ❤A Beautiful Journey Part II: Journaling to Self-Identity

- ❤Affirmations for a Beautiful Heart set 2

Fall 2024
- ❤A Heart for the Home Part III Adulthood: Mending every area of Brokenness in my Relationships

- ❤A Beautiful Journey Part III: Journaling to Mindfulness

- ❤Affirmations for a Beautiful Heart set 3

To enhance your resources, check out our MBBB Branded stationery products available ONLY at our website: www.ShariseAntionette.com

- ❤Glitter Diamond Top ink pens
- ❤Glitter Scissors
- ❤Resin Luxury Bookmarks
- ❤Resin Luxury Coasters
- ❤Resin Luxury Affirmation Card holders
- ❤Elegant Glitter Mugs
- ❤Affirmation Cards
- ❤Special Keepsake Boxes

Programs & Services

We are now serving authors and course creators who would like to add a workbook, journal, or set of affirmation cards to their brand. If your content is sinful or coming directly against Christianity or Jesus Christ, you automatically do not qualify and will be politely turned down. ********This only applies to our formatting services because we will be associated with our clients brand and content.********

- ❤Full Design, Layout, Structure, Cover Spread, and Format
- ❤Weekly LIVE clarity meeting and updates (up to 6 weeks)
- ❤Up to 6 changes, edits, and special request
- ❤1-on-1 Info meeting (Acceptance, approval, and qualification)
- ❤Design interpretation within 7 days of Approval
- ❤Careful attention to details and our client's vision
- ❤Quick production time
- ❤Estimation quote and time frame

Becoming More Beautiful is our signature program serving housewives who want to become homemakers. We will be discussing how to build intimacy in 4 categories of relationships; People, Your Self, Business, and Priorities, especially in the current season of your life.

- ❤12 week coaching program
- ❤12 LIVE sessions
- ❤12 LIVE Q & A's
- ❤Sisterhood and Private Community
- ❤Special Guest and Master Mentor Sessions
- ❤Graduation Ceremony

❤❤ ❤All Programs and services may be found and applied to ONLY at our website: www.ShariseAntionette.com ❤❤❤

Get Your Companion Journal Today!
Stay Tuned for the new releases of Part II and III . . .

A Companion Journal to: A Heart for the Hurt Series

A Beautiful Journey

Part I: A Journal to Healing

By: Sharise A. Caldwell

www.ingramcontent.com/pod-product-compliance
Lightning Source LLC
Chambersburg PA
CBHW070945120626
46546CB00004B/1579